Samuel J. May

A Brief Account of His Ministry

Given in a discourse, preached to the Church of the Messiah, in Syracuse,

N.Y., September 15th, 1867

Samuel J. May

A Brief Account of His Ministry
Given in a discourse, preached to the Church of the Messiah, in Syracuse, N.Y.,
September 15th, 1867

ISBN/EAN: 9783337290467

Printed in Europe, USA, Canada, Australia, Japan

Cover: Foto ©Lupo / pixelio.de

More available books at **www.hansebooks.com**

A BRIEF ACCOUNT OF HIS MINISTRY,

A DISCOURSE,

PREACHED TO THE

CHURCH OF THE MESSIAH,

IN

SYRACUSE, N. Y.,

September 15th, 1867,

BY SAMUEL J. MAY.

————•——

MASTERS & LEE, BOOK AND JOB PRINTERS.
1867.

SYRACUSE, Sept. 16, 1867.

REV. SAMUEL J. MAY,

Dear Sir :

Your Discourse of yesterday morning, on the occasion of your reaching the age of "threescore years and ten," was of so much interest to ourselves, that we are sure many persons, who did not hear it, would be greatly interested in its perusal.

May we ask you, then, to furnish it to us for publication, and by so doing, confer a favor upon them as well, as upon

Your Friends and Parishioners,

D. P. PHELPS,
E. B. JUDSON,
H. R. PHELPS,
H. N. GOODMAN,
CHAS. B. SEDGWICK,
E. B. CULVER,
H. P. STARK,
J. F. WILKINSON,
C. C. LOOMIS,
J. L. BAGG,
LYMAN CLARY,
GEO. GOODRICH,
O. T. BURT.

DISCOURSE.

Psalm xc. v. 20.—" THE DAYS OF OUR YEARS ARE THREESCORE YEARS AND TEN ; AND IF BY REASON OF STRENGTH, THEY BE FOURSCORE YEARS, YET IS THEIR STRENGTH LABOR AND SORROW."

Eight or ten years ago, I received from the Editor of a New York Periodical, the request, that I would write a sketch of my life for publication in his Monthly; or else furnish him with the materials for such a sketch. I replied that although the life of S. J. M. had been to *me* the most interesting and important of any life, ever spent on earth, I doubted whether a biography of it would be worthy the attention of the public; and therefore I must refuse to comply with his request.

But now that I have come so near to the termination of my temporal course; have attained that elevated point of observation, towards which I have been clambering these seventy years, the inclination to look back is irresistible; to survey the past; to review my life; to recall the incidents that made any particular impression upon my character, or gave any important turn to the course I have pursued; to think gratefully of the persons, whose influence has been salutary to me; to re-consider the opinions and principles I have been led to adopt and advocate; in a word, to pass some judgment on the result, to myself

and others, of what I have said, done, been, during
my seventy years. Especially in the pulpit, on the
Lord's day, am I impelled most anxiously to consider
what has been the prevailing character of my work
as a Christian minister; and what its value may have
been to my fellow men. Very nearly the half of that
work has been done in connection with this Church;
and as I have some confessions to make, and some
favors to ask of you to-day, dear friends, it is right
and proper, that you should be informed of the circumstances and influences, that led me to become such
a minister as I have been to you.

The 18th day of next December, it will be forty-
seven years, since I was examined by the Boston Association of Ministers, and received their approbation
as a candidate for the Christian Ministry. The following Sunday, Dec, 24th, I preached in Springfield
for my particular friend, Rev. W. B. O. Peabody. It
is not an insignificant fact in my history, that, though
in the trepidation of the moment, my voice must have
been very little "like a trumpet," I read in the morning service, the 58th chapter of Isaiah. I know not
what prompted me to do so, unless it may have been
the impressive words on Slavery, uttered a few days
before at Plymouth, by Daniel Webster, whom I then
revered more than any of our statesmen.

At that time, 1820, the controversy between the
supporters and opposers of the Calvinistic Theology
was at its height. One of the Episcopal, and all but
one of the Congregational Churches in Boston, had
renounced the horrible doctrines of the Genevan Re-
former. And the majority of the churches, within
thirty miles of that city, had done likewise. Unitarianism, as their new faith came to be called, was de-

cidedly in the ascendant in that region. And is it not a fact of very great significance, that just there, where alone in all the world Unitarian views of re-ligion have ever been in the ascendant, in that very community, nearly all of the benevolent and philan-thropic enterprises, that have signalized the last sixty years of our nation's history, were devised; and there have found many of their most zealous promoters.*

My parents were members of the first avowed Uni-tarian Church in America, which had been the first Episcopal Church† in New England. They did not think that true religion subsisted in the belief of any system of dogmas, however venerable, nor in the ob-servance of ceremonies, however solemn; but in per-sonal godliness, in loving the Heavenly Father, and evincing that love by kindnesses to his earthly family, our fellow beings; by doing justly, loving mercy and walking humbly; visiting the fatherless and widows in their affliction, and keeping oneself unspotted from the world; reverencing God, and keeping his com-mandments; looking unto " the dearly beloved son" as the mark of our high calling, and striving to be-come like him.

Accordingly they educated me and all their chil-dren *religiously* rather than *theologically*. They taught us of God from the wonderful and beautiful works of his creation, and the dispensations of his providence; and in the impressive lessons of the Bible. They taught us of Jesus Christ, and of the nature, the du-ties and the destiny of man, from the intelligible, interesting, devotional portions of the Old Testament; but mainly from the Four Gospels and the Acts of the Apostles; more especially from the words and

---

* See Appendix, " A." † The King's Chapel, See Appendix, "B."

life of Jesus himself. All *his* precepts it was enjoined upon us to obey; and the beauties and graces of
his character were continually held up to be admired
and imitated. Whatever was wrong, untruthful, de-
ceitful, unkind, selfish, sensual, profane, impure, our
parents strove to make us see was mean, unworthy of
us as moral beings, not less than offensive to them and
most of all offensive to our Father in Heaven. They
took great pains to keep alive in us the sense of ac-
countability — of a future as well as a present retri-
bution. The assurance of our immortality, of enter-
ing through death into a higher life, (a far happier,
an angelic life to the good,) was most assiduously
given me, before I was six years old, under circumstances, and in a manner, that fixed that truth among
the deepest roots of my being. It was given to con-
sole me, and allay my passionate grief, for the death
of my almost twin brother, whom I loved more than
any body but my mother, and who was killed by an
accident while we were playing together. Ever since
then, my belief that mortals shall live again after
death, has been about as strong as my consciousness
of present existence.

In our religious education, my parents made some
use of a very simple Catechism, prepared by our minister, but relied mainly upon the devotional and pre-
ceptive parts of the Old and New Testaments. I
therefore knew nothing, had never heard, of the heart-
withering theology of St. Augustine and Calvin,
which had so long been taught in most of the churches
as Christianity, until I was old enough to take an interest in the discussions on the subject, that became
frequent about the year 1810. It was not however,
until 1815, that the Unitarian Controversy, so called,

was fully broached. At that time I was in the midst
of my college course; and was too much engrossed by
classical and scientific studies, to give much attention
to any other subjects. In the Fall of 1817, therefore,
I entered upon my theological studies, with no germ
of a system of Faith in my mind, other than such as
you may suppose I had derived from the simple,
scriptural instructions given me by my parents.

The following six months I studied under the direction of Rev. Henry Colman of Hingham, at the
same time assisting him in a Classical school, which
he was then keeping. Mr. Colman was an active,
enterprising, genial man and minister, esteeming practical Christianity more highly than that, which was
mainly doctrinal and ceremonial. *Theological*

In the Spring of 1818, I entered the Divinity School
at Cambridge, in which the instructions, for the most
part, then were given by the wise, liberal, devout Dr.
Ware, Sen., the learned, astute, conscientious Andrews
Norton; together with admirable lectures and con-
versations on Moral Philosophy by Prof. Frisbie; and
lessons in the Hebrew language by Prof. Willard.
These gentlemen marked out for us a sufficiently extended theological, as well as ethical and devotional
course of reading; but they peremptorily *dictated* nothing except personal purity and righteousness, the dili-
gent improvement of our advantages, and fidelity to
our highest sense of the true and the right. They
enjoined it upon us to examine every subject, brought
to our consideration, thoroughly, as impartially as we
were able to, in the various lights thrown upon it by
the religious and theological writers of opposite sects,
and to accept such conclusions as should, after such
an examination, seem to our own minds correct—ever

remembering our responsibility to God alone* for the use we made of our opportunities to learn, and of the powers He had given us to judge of the true and the right.

Thus encouraged I entered upon the inquiry after *true Religion*, fully persuaded that it was the "one thing needful" for all men; and longing to be a minister of it to my fellow beings, so many of whom seemed to me to be "living without God in the world."

I was soon more than ever convinced, that Christianity was the true religion; but that a strange theology had been foisted into its place in Christendom; substituted for it in most of the churches. It seemed to me self-evident, that Christianity was to be learnt from Jesus Christ; that he must be the best teacher of his own Religion; that, if he be, as most Christians profess to regard him, "the author and *finisher* of our faith," nothing should be *appended* to the Gospel as he left it; not even on the authority of Paul, Apollos, or Cephas, certainly not on the authority of St. Augustine, John Calvin, or the Pope, should any thing be prescribed as essential, which is not perfectly consistent with the teachings of the Master. It seemed to me then, as it seems to me now, the highest impertinence, egregious presumption, in any Doctor of Divinity, or Assembly of Divines, (especially those who believe that Jesus was a super-human being, aye, the very God,) to prescribe a Creed, as comprising the essential faith, which is no where to be found in the words of the Master. Can any one doubt, if the belief in such a system of dogmas as the Presbyterian Confession of Faith, or the Creeds and Thirty-nine

* See Appendix, "C."

Articles of the Episcopal Church, were essential to human salvation, that the Savior of mankind would have left a distinct statement of them; given them the sanction of his authority? What an imputation it is upon the divinely appointed teacher of true Religion, that he left his work so imperfectly done, as to make it necessary for Popes and Bishops and Ecclesiastical Councils to improve it — to state more distinctly the essential articles of faith, and even to re-construct the whole system!

When I first read the Presbyterian Confession of Faith, and the Thirty-nine Articles of the Episcopal Church, I was shocked, I was horrified by the doctrines therein set forth — implying that God is the most unreasonable, cruel, relentless tyrant; and the whole human race born under the curse of God, doomed to everlasting, inconceivably awful suffering, from which they can do nothing to deliver themselves; nay, from which it was decreed before the foundation of the world, that only a very small fraction of the children of men — the elect — should be delivered, although the "very God" himself had given his life to redeem them. I say, I was so shocked, horrified at this Theology, which assumed to be orthodox, that I was unspeakably comforted by not finding it in the Bible, certainly not in any of the teachings of Jesus Christ. And, not withstanding the fact that this Theology had been, for centuries, so generally accepted and taught in the so called Christian churches, I could not but regard it as an utter corruption of Christianity; and I felt all the more eager to go forth, and do all that the God of truth might enable me to do, to dispel this dense, dark cloud of error from the face of " the Sun of righteousness."

From the first, it was deeply impressed upon my heart, that a minister of the Gospel ought not to choose his place of labor, influenced by any considerations of ease, pecuniary profit, or professional distinction; but that he should go withersoever the finger of Providence seemed plainly to direct him. I thought it would be wise in a young man to defer the responsibilities of a settled ministry, until he had had some experience in the labors of the pulpit, and had learnt as much as he might by observation and inquiry of parochial duties. I therefore declined an urgent invitation to settle in Brooklyn, Conn. received in April, 1821; and the following September, discouraged an invitation that, I was told by the Committee, awaited me to settle as minister of the first Unitarian Church in New York City. I had preached to that church seven or eight Sundays on two engagements in the course of the Summer, and had become much interested in their welfare. But at the time I received their invitation to return to them again, I had just entered upon a second engagement to serve, for three months, as Dr. Channing's assistant. Assured that it would be an inestimable benefit to me to be so associated with that eminent divine, I declined the invitation to return to New York then; and before the expiration of three months the church there had engaged the Rev. William Ware to become their pastor.

Between my two terms of preaching in New York, the former in May, the latter in July, 1821, I visited Baltimore, Washington, Alexandria and Richmond. Then it was—in those cities, and in the countries between them, that, for the first time, I saw portions of the *enslaved* population of the land. Then it was, that their wrongs were brought home to me; the iron of their chains entered into my soul. I hoped, I longed to do someting for their deliverance. What could be done, I did not plainly see. Our nation had (only the year before) put a new rivet into their shackles— the *Missouri Compromise* — and had given to their oppressors a new guarantee. I rested in the assurance that such a system of iniquity must be, would be subverted; and that when the time came, I should have a hand in its overthrow.*

My connection with Dr. Channing continued until the close of the year. It was, as you may well suppose it must have been, eminently beneficial to me in several respects; and it laid the foundation of a friendship, which was cherished with unabated ardor, on my part, until the close of his saint-like life.

During my visit to Baltimore, in the Summer of 1821, I staid in the family of a relative, with whom that eminent scholar, historian and champion of liberal Christianity — the late Rev. Dr. Sparks, then resided. He was assiduously devoted to the dissemination of rational, practical religion. On my return from Richmond, we conferred together as to the feasibility of gathering a Unitarian Church in the capital of Virginia, where I knew a few, and he knew more persons inclined to Christianity rather than Calvinism.

The following January I received a letter from him, in which he proposed, that so soon as his duties to Congress, of which body he was then the Chaplain, should cease, I should supply his pulpit in Baltimore several Sundays, which he would spend in Richmond, gathering together as many as he might find there, disposed to unite in a Unitarian Church. And, on his

---

* See Appendix "D."

return, if sufficient encouragement should be given him, I should go to that city, and carry on the work he had commenced. To this proposal I at once acceded; and set about making the best preparation I could for the undertaking, in the lively belief, that that was the part of the vineyard, to which the finger of Providence was directing me.

Near the close of February, I received another letter from Mr. Sparks, informing me that after the 4th of March, he should be at liberty to commence our proposed attempt on Richmond, and requesting me to come on without delay. I had just started for the post-office, with my answer, that I would be in Baltimore before the close of the ensuing week, when lo! a committee met me at the door—two excellent, earnest gentlemen from Brooklyn, Connecticut, who had come to invite, persuade, compel me to become the minister of the church there, to which I had preached the year before, and whose earnest invitation then, I had refused, on the ground of inexperience. They were men not to be easily diverted from their purpose.

The history of the church, they plead for, was interesting, and its circumstances were trying. Their junior pastor, Rev. Luther Wilson, a man of free spirit, and an earnest inquirer after truth, not being satisfied with the dogmas of Orthodoxy, was attracted to Boston in 1815, by what he heard of the controversy then at its height. He went thither: became acquainted with Dr. Channing, Dr. Noah Worcester and other confessors of the Unitarian faith; obtained the best publications then extant, and soon became converted to "the new heresy," as it was called. He soon found that many of the leading members of the church in Brooklyn were ready to receive the more rational, and scriptural views of God, Christ and human nature, to which he had been led. At once the orthodox portion attempted to eject him from his pastorate, although they alleged nothing against him excepting this change in his theological opinions, his reasons for which, they would not listen to. Finding that a Mutual Council would not advise his dismission, the minority of the Church called to their aid the Consociation of Windham County, once a powerful ecclesiastical body. It was doubtful whether their jurisdiction extended over this Brooklyn Church, which was one of a number of Churches, that, on a former occasion, had declared their independence, and their preference for the Congregational mode of church government. Nevertheless the Consociation proceeded to try Mr. Wilson for heresy. Of course they found him guilty. So they declared him unfit to be a christian minister, and pronounced his connection with the Brooklyn Church, dissolved. Mr. Wilson yielded, under protest, to the decision, and was soon installed in Petersham, Mass., in 1820. But his friends, being a majority of the parish, retained the meeting-house, and the name of the "First Ecclesiastical Society in Brooklyn."

Several candidates had been invited to take the place, thus opened in Connecticut, for a Unitarian Minister. But all had refused. So, in their despair, they appealed to me again. And I could not withstand their appeal. They had come to me in behalf of the only Unitarian Church in that State. They reprerented a body, who were striving, at a fearful odds, to maintain not only theological opinions, that I deemed very important, but to vindicate the fundamental

14

principles of Religious Liberty. The deepest conviction was awakened in my bosom, that it was my duty to accept the Call; that the finger of Providence did indeed point distinctly to Brooklyn as the sphere, in which I was to labor. So I consented.

My parents and friends all remonstrated against the decision. I should go there, they said, to encounter alone the opposition of the Orthodoxy of the whole Commonwealth; far away as it then was, (before Railroads were invented,) from clerical fathers and brothers, with whom I could take counsel, and from whom I might receive sympathy and aid. I should be obliged moreover, they urged, to live on a wholly insufficient salary; perhaps to struggle with poverty. But their remonstrances did not reach to the depth of my conviction, that I ought to go. Accordingly I turned away from Richmond, and from another inviting place, in which I might have been settled, and set my face towards Brooklyn. On the 13th of March, 1822, I was ordained; and the following Sunday commenced my ministry there.

Forever shall I bless the Father of my spirit, that he sent me to that place. I was there introduced to new and most profitable experiences—to the society of industrious, staid, sensible, skilful, independent farmers. All the gentlemen in the town, excepting four lawyers, two physicians, three clergymen, the sheriff, jailor and clerk of the court (for it was the shire town,) three merchants and three tavern-keepers, got their living by labor on their lands, or in those handicrafts, that are indispensable in every community. And all the ladies, however well educated and refined, took the lead in the work of their households and of their dairies. So the dainty notions and conventional·

isms, that I had acquired in city life, were put to flight. The deep meaning of Burns' famous song, "a man's a man for a' that and a' that," was revealed to my soul; and I learnt to respect a hman being for his humanity, and his character, and not because of his accidents or circumstances.

It was in Brooklyn that I learnt, by experience, how little else a man needs to support and comfort him, if he has the consciousness of loving the true, and obeying the right. Some of my opinions, other than theological, were quite new and accounted strange in that community. While at Cambridge, in my Senior year, and during my course in the Divinity School, I became rather intimately acquainted with the venerable Dr. Noah Worcester, one of the earliest confessors of Unitarianism. He was a saint. Like Enoch of old, "he walked with God." He was a peace-maker. The last twenty years of his life were assiduously devoted to the cause of Peace. He corresponded on the subject with prominent men in all parts of Christendom; and he conducted for several years a periodical devoted to the cause. His "Solemn Review of the custom of war," is the most complete exposure of the folly, and the most impressive testimony to the wickedness of War, that I have ever heard or read. I do not believe that any one can read it attentively, and not be convinced, that it is impossible to conduct a war, offensive or defensive, on Christian principles, or in a Christian spirit. I was so affected by the writings and the heavenly conversation of Dr. Worcester, that soon after my settlement, I commenced enjoining upon my congregation, obedience to the pacific precepts of Jesus. The first Sermon I ever published was on the "Treatment of Enemies, prescribed by Christianity." And two or three years after my settlement, I had succeeded in organizing the Windham County Peace Society, which comprised ministers and laymen of all denominations.*

Another reform was commenced in Boston in 1815, which seemed to me greatly needed—the suppression of the vice of Intemperance. Statistics of the evils caused by the use of intoxicating drinks, were diligently gathered up and spread before the people in elaborate reports, and pressed upon their consideration in eloquent addresses and sermons. But the effects produced were far less, than the alarming condition of the community demanded. The friends of the cause were surprised at the public apathy. Some were discouraged. I happened to be at a business meeting of the "Massachusetts Society for the suppression of Intemperance," in May, 1826. It was held in the large Vestry of "the First Church" in Boston. We had just been listening, in the Meeting-house above, to a very pertinent and impressive address by Dr. John Ware, adapted to awaken in every bosom the deepest solicitude. The question naturally pressed itself upon us, what more shall we do—what more can be done, to stay the progress of this desolating vice? Several propositions had been made by one and another, when Dr. Lowell of the West Church, arose, and, with a solemnity which would have been awful, if it had not been attempered by his wonted, almost maternal tenderness, said, "Brethren, we have not struck deep enough to extirpate this dreadful vice. Intemperate persons cannot use moderately, that which is intoxicating. We must persuade them to abstain wholly from such drinks. To do this, we

---

* See Appendix, "E."

must abstain ourselves: banish the use of all such liquors from our tables; touch not, taste not, handle not." My heart—with the hearts of many who were present, responded fully to his demand. A similar conviction seems to have been awakened in other bosoms at that time. For the American Total Abstinence Society was formed that year, and for awhile seemed to be the instrument, by which the reform, we so much desired, was to be effected.

Inspired with new zeal, I hastened back to my home and my church. My precious wife cordially embraced the principle of total abstinence. We consigned a hamper of delicious wine, just received from a friend in Boston, to the service of the sick; I emptied my cider barrel into the vinegar cask; and we treated our guests to cake and cold water. I at once proclaimed the doctrine from my pulpit. It was generally accepted. All the facts of the case in Brooklyn, were ferreted out, and shown to sustain the awful statistics of the Temperance Societies. It was found that we had in our midst our proportion of the evils produced by intoxicating drink. A town Society was soon formed and the cause of temperance prospered.[*]

Soon after my settlement in Brooklyn, I was chosen one of the School Committee, or Board of Education, and continued in the office so long as I resided there. When I came into Connecticut, it was with the expectation that I should find her Common Schools far in advance of ours in Massachusetts, or in any other part of our country. In 1794, her Legislature passed an Act, giving the proceeds of the sales of her western lands, amounting to *four million of dollars*, to the cause of popular education. It was a glorious deed,

---

[*] See Appendix, "F."

for which the doers of it ought forever to be honored. It evinced too, the prevalence of a sentiment among their constituents, on the subject of public instruction, which deservedly, at the time, placed that Commonwealth high in the esteem of the friends of Republican Institutions, which can be well sustained only by an intelligent population. But I had not been long in Connecticut, before I discovered, that the condition of her schools was lower than the corresponding schools of Massachusetts. The cause of this was soon discovered. For a number of years after the creation of the School Fund, the income from that source was sufficient to support the common schools as they then were, and the people were exonerated from much, if not any taxation on their account. But as the population of the State had doubled, and the number of schools had increased almost in the same proportion, the income, though greater, was quite insufficient to support so many, and such schools, as the due instruction of the children of the State required. Yet the people, not having been used to making appropriations for education, were reluctant to do so. And as they paid nothing for the schools, they cared little about them. The wages offered to teachers were not high enough to command the services of competent ones, so that the instructions given by many of them were meagre and inaccurate. So general was this found to be the condition of the public schools of Connecticut, that several friends of education in other towns united with our Brooklyn committee in calling a State Convention in October, 1827, to consider this matter of paramount importance. It was well attended, and was doubtless the beginning of a great reformation. The revelation that was made of the low estate of the schools, almost every where, surprised and mortified the people, and disposed them to favor plans of improvement.*

In Oct. 1830, I was providentially in Boston, to hear William Loyd Garrison's first lectures on American Slavery, which then assumed to be the dominant Institution of our Republic. He depicted as no other one had done, the wrongs and sufferings of enslaved millions in our land. He demonstrated the almost unparalleled iniquity, of those who were holding human beings in the condition of domesticated brutes; and the guilt of our Nation in consenting to their oppression. He exposed the real spirit and purpose of the Colonization Scheme, which was then rapidly gaining favor with the northern philanthropists. And he insisted, that immediate emancipation, without removal from the country, or the spot on which he dwelt, was the right of every slave, and the duty of his master. The hearing of those lectures was an epoch in my life, having, more than any other event, given direction and character to my course as a citizen and a minister.†

I carried home his doctrines to my church in Brooklyn; and I am proud to record, that all but two or three of the members embraced them at once. They welcomed Mr. Garrison and other anti-slavery lecturers to my pulpit; and heartily co-operated with me in my endeavors to disseminate the doctrines throughout that region. They justified me in my espousal of the cause of that noble woman, Prudence Crandall, and helped me to maintain a struggle for two years in defence of her right to keep her "school in Canterbury, for colored girls." The arguments that were

---

* See Appendix "G."   † See Appendix, "H."

made in Court in this case; the discussions to which
it gave rise in the newspapers, and in the meetings of
the Colonization and Anti-Slavery Societies; and the
lectures that were delivered in almost every town, so
instructed the people, and elevated their sentiments,
that Windham has been since 1833, the leading County in Connecticut on all questions pertaining to the
Rights of Man. Last year, that county gave the largest, if not the only majority vote for *impartial suf-
frage*—the enfranchisement of colored men.*
Much as my time and thoughts, in the first years of
my ministry, were given to Peace, Temperance, Popular Education, and the Abolition of Slavery, I endeav-
ored to do my duties as a pastor, and as a preacher of
the Christian Religion. My situation was lonely, my
duties arduous, and my perplexities were sometimes
great. But from all these I derived a mental and
moral discipline, not to be had in Divinity Schools,
nor under the controlling influence of Ecclesiastic or
Ministerial Associations. I felt bound to take my
stand, not as the partizan of any Sect, nor as the de-
fender of any Theological System, or any church us-
ages; but as a Minister, a servant whose duty it was
to persuade my fellow men to come to my Master,
Jesus Christ, and learn of him. I insisted that no
man nor body of men; no church nor consociation of
churches; no presbytery, synod nor general assembly;
no bishop nor bench of bishops; no college of card-
inals nor the Pope had the least authority given them
by God or Christ to *dictate* to the humblest individual what he *shall believe*. They might advise, instruct,
argue with him; but they might not *dictate*, without
being guilty of high presumption. God requires of us,

* See Anti-Slavery Recollections.

we may require of each other, therefore churches, consociations, synods, bishops, popes may require of each individual, who acknowledges the authority of either, that he shall be *good*, and do *good;* that he shall believe that, which will induce him to reverence God, and keep his commandments. And, wherever it is obvious in the life and conversation of any one, that he does believe that, which has induced him " to deny ungodliness and worldly lusts, and to live soberly, righteously and godly in the world," there are we all bound to consent, all churches and ecclesiastical bodies of every name are bound to consent, that that man has a faith, which is *unto salvation*, whether it accords, or not, with the creeds or articles of any sect.

This radical position I took, and stated, with the utmost plainness, and maintained, as ably as I could. Few of my orthodox neighbors came to hear me, or were converted, if they did venture to hear. But many of them treated me courteously; and some became my personal friends, and hearty fellow laborers in several christian works. So that I learnt that an orthodox man can be " a man for 'a that and 'a that."

I soon found, that there was still lingering among the members of my Church not a little superstition respecting the Lord's Supper, an ordinance in which I then took and still take delight. Many of them regarded it as an especially sacred and solemn ceremony, for which particular preparation should be made. They were therefore inclined to have the Preparatory Lecture on the Thursday preceding each Communion Sunday. I questioned the propriety of making such a distinction. I insisted, that it was no more a sacrament than public prayer: indeed, that a direct address to God was the most solemn act, that a mortal being

could engage in; and that special preparation of mind
and heart for public worship, for engaging in the
prayers and hymns of the Lord's day, was just as
needful, as for the observance of the Lord's Supper.
I said to them, I am willing to give every Thursday
a lecture preparatory to the services of the following
Sunday; but I am not willing to make such a distinction of the Communion Sunday; for I am sure, that
he, who joins in the prayers or the hymns of the
Lord's day unworthily, doeth it to his condemnation,
just as much as he, who eateth and drinketh at the
Lord's table unworthily; aye, more so, for in the former act he insults the Heavenly Father; in the latter
act he insults the Son, and we have the assurance of
Jesus himself (Matt. xii, 32,) that the former is much
the less pardonable offence. After due consideration
the Church consented to the change.

Again, I observed that an aged member of the
Church—acknowledged to be one of the best men in
it—always remained, and very reverently witnessed
the Lord's Supper, but never partook of it. I enquir-
ed the reason. He informed me, that he considered
baptism to be a necessary pre-requisite; and that he
regarded *immersion* as the only true baptism. But
he had been sprinkled in infancy, at the request of his
parents, and therefore the ministers hitherto had refused to baptize him again. I replied, if you do not
believe in infant baptism, and are not satisfied with
sprinkling, then the ordinance ought to be administered to you by immersion; and I am ready at any
time to render you that service; for baptism was made
for man, and not man for baptism. He replied, that
he should esteem it a great privilege to partake of the
Lord's Supper; but he did not wish me to do any

thing for his sake, that would be accounted disorderly or irregular. "You are a young man," said he, "and had better not depart from what has been customary in the churches." His humility made me all the more determined to secure to him the privilege he esteemed so highly. So I wrote letters to two aged ministers in Massachusetts, stating the case, and asking their advice. Greatly to my disappointment, they gave it as their opinion, that I had better not do what would imply the insufficiency of sprinkling, or of infant baptism; but adhere to the usage of the Congregational churches, and do what I could to convince my friend of the sufficiency of his parents' act, or else to reconcile him to his deprivation.

In vain I tried to convince him; and the more he was reconciled to his privation, the less could I reconcile myself to it. On the first Sunday of every month, the good man took his seat near the communicants, but denied himself any portion of the bread and the wine. I endured the sight nearly a year, and then insisted upon removing the barrier, that kept him from full communion with us. I felt that the rights and feelings of a good man, were more to be respected than the usage of the Church.

So the time for the public baptism of Mr. W. was announced. The place was appropiate and beautiful. It was the broad bend of Blackwell's brook, where there was a clean, pebbly beach, in the middle of an extensive meadow of fresh mown grass. It was a bright Summer, quiet Sunday afternoon. The assembly to witness the ceremony was large. I had never so administered the rite but once before; nor had I ever seen it so administered by another. Of course, I was somewhat agitated, as was the recipient. The spectators were deeply affected; so much more so than I had ever seen them to be at other baptisms, that, on coming up out of the water, I felt it my duty to admonish them, that the efficacy of the rite did not inhere in the mode of its administration, but in the purpose and spirit of him who submitted to it. One drop of water, I said, would be sufficient for one, who sincerely intended to become a disciple of Jesus; an ocean of water would not be enough to baptize truly a pretender.

This case of Mr. W.'s led to much thought on the origin, design and use of the Lord's Supper. Ere long I became convinced, that no portion of a Church had a right to appropriate it to themselves; to set up barriers around it; to forbid any to approach it but those, who would subscribe to their creed, or comply with such conditions as they should impose. It seemed to me not an end, but a means; not the consummation of the Christian's course, but a help to attain it. I could no longer consider it as any more than one of "the means of grace." Therefore that every person who felt the need of it, or believed in, and desired its efficacy, had as much right to it as to the benefits of "the word" dispensed from the pulpit, or the influence of the prayers offered by the congregation. In due time I persuaded "the Communicants" of that Church, that it would be right to proffer that sacrament to all their fellow worshippers. And, for several years before I left Brooklyn, I was permitted, on Communion days, to invite all to partake of the Lord's Supper, "who felt their obligations to Jesus Christ, and were gratefully and devoutly disposed to commemorate his death."

Early in the year 1828, I received a letter from a

number of gentlemen in Providence, R. I. requesting me to come to that city, and attempt the formation of a second Unitarian Church. I went and preached four Sundays in the Old Richmond St. Meeting-house, recently vacated for a new one, by an Orthodox Society. After my last Sunday's service, I assisted at the organization of what has since been called the Westminster Church: and received an invitation, signed by eighty-two adults, to become their pastor.

The inducements to accept this call were very strong. The Church in Brooklyn was still small. My labors for six years had added not more than a dozen families to the original number. The soil of Connecticut was so saturated with Calvinism, that it was most ungenial to the true vine. My salary hitherto had been insufficient, and was becoming more so. Brooklyn was so situated, that it was not likely to increase much in population. Whereas Providence was a growing, thriving city; and the individuals, who had formed the new Church, were among the most intelligent, earnest, enterprising of the citizens.

These considerations inclined me not a little to accept their invitation. My conscientious wife persistently refused to influence my decision either way. "You know, or should know your duty," she would say, " better than I, or any one else can know it. All that I desire is that you should do what, you may be fully persuaded, you ought to do. It shall never be said, that to gratify your wife, you remained here or removed."

So soon as it was made known to the Church, that I had received a Call to Providence, the members, with one accord, entreated me not to leave them. They pressed upon my consideration the disastrous effects of my removal, not only upon their small, devoted, isolat-

ed band; but upon liberal and rational Christianity
in the State. And they generously promised to do
all in their power to make my means of living ade·
quate. Again their arguments and their urgency prevailed. I declined the invitation to Providence, and
at the request of the new Church went to Cambridge,
and selected Rev. F. A. now Dr. Farley of Brooklyn,
N. Y. to be their minister. Thus have they been fav·
ored from the beginning by the services of eminent
men, Rev. Dr. Osgood, now of New York, Rev. Dr.
Hedge of Brookline, Mass. having succeeded Dr. Farley, and the Rev. A Woodbury being the present in·
cumbent.

In accordance with their promises of help in the
way of living, my faithful Brooklyn friends soon after
set about to enable me to have a house of my own.
One offered me a very desirable site, with land enough
for a garden, and orchard. Others promised to con·
tribute all the timber and building materials, that they
could procure from their farms. And others engaged
to dig and stone my cellar and my well; and surround
my lot with substantial stone fences. All this, in due
time, they did, so that I was put in possession of
" a home, sweet home," which, as real estate, was worth
nearly $2000, and for which I paid by the help of my
father only about $800. Then I thought I was indeed
settled for life; satisfied myself that that was the
place, in which it was designed I should labor to the
end: and so I went to the pretty cemetry, a half mile
below the village, and selected the spot where I would
have my remains deposited, whenever my work on
earth should be done.

In 1831, however, I was invited to preach in Hart·
ford, Conn., and attempt the formation of a Unitarian

Church in that city. The moving spirits in the enter-
prise, were James H. Wells, Esq. and his wife: he a
well educated, refined, wise gentleman, of the highest
personal and social character; she in these respects
his equal: and surpassing him somewhat in religious
zeal. They were born in England of Unitarian parents; his father a minister of that denomination; and
they had come to feel deeply the want, for their children's sake more than their own, of a truer dispensation
of the Gospel, than they could expect from any of the
pulpits in Hartford—Dr. Bushnell then having hardly
commenced his work. Accordingly I went, resided
several weeks in their interesting family, and preached
to good and increasing audiences. The nucleus of a
church was formed; the lot for a Meeting-house was
purchased; and the plan of the building was drawn;
when the alarming and protracted sickness of their
son at a distance from home required their long continued absence; and, on their return, untoward circumstances in business made it advisable to postpone the
undertaking indefinitely. So I returned to my loved
home, and small but interesting charge in Brooklyn,
still more fully persuaded that that was the place as-
signed me in the vineyard of the Lord.*

But in the Summer of 1834, I felt it to be my
duty to leave the Church of Brooklyn for several
weeks, that I might accept many invitations to lecture
on the subject of American Slavery. Again, in the
Spring of 1835, I left them for a year or more, to become the General Agent and Corresponding Secretary
of the Massachusetts Anti-Slavery Society. A nar-
rative of my experiences, during the fourteen months

---

* See Appendix, "L."

that I occupied that position, would be too long for this occasion.*

On my return to Brooklyn in June, 1836, I found that a considerable number of my former parishioners had emigrated to Indiana, seriously lessening the ability of the Church to pay the scanty salary, on which I had been before barely able to subsist with my family. We therefore reluctantly dissolved our connection ;† and on the 26th of the following October, I was installed as pastor of the Church of South Scituate, Mass. I was first known there as an anti-slavery lecturer. So the people knew what to expect. Nevertheless, only two persons voted against my settlement; and a large portion of the Society ere long became Abolitionists.

Here also I made great and very successful efforts in the cause of temperance. The drinking customs of society were about the same there as elsewhere in our country, and many of the good people of the town were sorrowing over the sins and the miseries caused by the prevalent indulgence. They therefore joined heartily in our measures of opposition, which were greatly blessed. In due time, the use of intoxicating drinks was banished from almost every family; the sale of them was discontinued at the stores and taverns; and several persons, who had been considered abandoned drunkards, were reclaimed and lived in sobriety to the end of their days.

This blessed change was effected mainly by the valor of the children and youth of the town, whom we banded together into a "*Cold Water Army.*" An Army it was, nearly five hundred strong, "an Army with banners," indeed, many beautiful significant ban-

* See Anti-Slavery Recollections.　　† See Appendix, "I."

ners; but with no other weapons than awful facts, affecting narratives, solemn warnings, earnest, prayerful appeals. These were wielded vigorously by the young soldiers, in speeches, recitations, songs and hymns. And they prevailed gloriously. The result was the indictment, public trial, and emphatic condemnation of Alcohol as a common nuisance, and an accessory to almost all the crimes and misdemeanors, that had disturbed the peace of the community, destroyed the happiness of families, degraded individuals to a condition lower than brutal, and every year brought more to untimely deaths than the most dire pestilence. Then followed the execution. It was had on a knoll in the midst of a beautiful meadow, in the presence of several hundreds of the adult citizens of the town, who had been escorted thither by the Cold Water Army in full force, with banners flying, inspirited and guided by appropriate music. The arch-enemy, robber, burglar, incendiary, murderer, all in one—represented by relics of Rum, Brandy, Wine, Cider and Beer, that we had bought of the last rumseller in town to close his accursed traffic,—had been dragged on a wagon in the procession to the appointed spot. And when the trial was over, the verdict given and the sentence pronounced, then the Executioners stepped forward, and, the command being given, despatched the culprit with well dealt blows, and poured his blood upon the ground. The effect was most impressive, and, as I have been assured, has never been effaced.

It was also while I lived in South Scituate, that I commenced my acquaintance with another of the greatest benefactors of our country, Horace Mann. He soon interested me deeply in his large, and well devised plans for the improvement of our System of Public Instruction; especially the institution of Normal Schools, for the thorough training of those, who would be teachers in our Common Schools. I co-operated with him to the extent of my ability, by lecturing on the subject in most of the towns of Plymouth County; and assisting at sundry Conventions of the people.

It was by Mr. Mann's persuasion that, after six of the happiest years of my life had passed at South Scituate,* I resigned my ministry there, and became the Principal of the State Normal School at Lexington, in place of Rev. Cyrus Pierce, who had inaugurated that admirable institution;† and had devoted himself to it with an assiduity, that nearly cost him his life.

Nothing reveals to one so clearly the amount and accuracy of his own knowledge, (or their opposites) so surely as his attempt to teach others properly. I found myself much less competent to meet several of the demands made upon me in that School, than I had supposed myself to be. I should not have retained the place a year, but for the all-sufficient assistance given me by Miss Caroline Tilden, who was unquestionably a *genius* in the art of teaching; and Miss Electa N. Lincoln, whose talents were so various and excellent, that they amounted almost to genius. Thus supported, I spared no pains to make the Institution what I knew it ought to be. I aspired to become a thorough Normal teacher. And as the *suitable* preparation of teachers for our common schools, had come to appear to me the most useful work, in which a man could be engaged, I should have continued in it, per-

* See Appendix "J."   † Now at Framingham.

haps until this day, if Mr. Pierce had not after two years of rest and recreation, unexpectedly recovered his health. Knowing, as I did full well, his unequelled qualifications for that office, I insisted upon resigning it to him; and returned to the ministry.

Indeed I had never left the ministry, for during much of the time, that I had charge of the Normal School, I preached on more than half of the Sundays in the neighboring towns, especially in East Lexington, a place endeared to me by its relations to my friend—the inestimable Dr. Follen.

So soon as it was known, that I was about to resign the School, I was invited to become the minister of the Church of old Lexington, and preach in the meeting house, that stood where the first battle in the war of the American Revolution was had; in the same enclosure with the monument erected to the memory of the patriots, who fell in that conflict.*

Parker is one of the names inscribed on that memorial stone. Parker was the name of the Captain, who commanded the company of seventy, that offered the first resistance to the British troops. He was grandfather of the man, whose name and fame have spread as far and wide as that of any of our cotemporaries. Theodore Parker was born in Lexington. And it was while I was the temporary minister of the church in that town, that the trouble occasioned by Mr. Parker's opinions came to its height in the Boston Association of Ministers. I was surprised at the course those gentlemen adopted. I was disconcerted. It seemed to me, that they had lost confidence in the fundamental principle of Liberal Christianity. Mr. Parker's doctrines were then, more than they are now, offen-

---

* See Appendix "K."

sive to me; as much so, probably, as they were to any of the Boston ministers. But they were not a tythe so offensive, so subversive of Christianity, as the doctrines of the Presbyterian and Episcopal Churches; and yet my Boston brethren did not, any more than myself, deny or doubt that there were some eminently religious preachers and persons, who avowed their faith in those orthodox theologies. If, then, we believed it possible for a Calvinist to be a good Christian, I saw not why we should doubt, that a Rationalist might be. So I determined to know more of the young heretic, with whom I was barely acquainted. I wished him to be assured, that I did not sympathise with those, who would virtually, if not formally, excommunicate him because of his opinions. I presumed that, in his doctrines, he did not differ from me, more than I differed from him; and I knew not what authority either of us had to condemn the other for his mode of faith. Accordingly I wrote him an invitation to exchange with me, and to spend a day with me, or allow me to spend it with him. My invitation was promptly and cordially accepted. I went to West Roxbury, where he was then settled, early on Saturday. We spent that afternoon and evening together. He returned from Lexington, early Sunday evening; and I did not leave him until Monday afternoon. So we had many hours of intimate communion of mind and heart. I could not assent to some of his opinions, nor did I convert him to mine. But I was filled with admiration of his various and extensive learning. I could not but respect his fearless frankness; and I caught some glimpses of the depths of his piety—and the warmth of his benevolence. Then commenced a friendship, which grew more and more

earnest and tender to the day of his death; a friendship which I trust, will survive the grave.

It was during my first summer vacation at Lexington, that I came out with my precious wife to visit
Niagara Falls, and give her and myself the recreation
of travel. At the request of my valued friend, the
Rev. Mr. Storer—your first and most excellent pastor,
I stopped in Syracuse on my way out, and again on
my return; and preached twice in your little Meeting-house on Genesee street.

Thus it was, dear Friends, that our acquaintance
commenced twenty-four years ago last month, which
led to my settlement with you in April, 1845, as your
minister. What sort of a minister I should probably
be, you were fairly warned, for during my visits, in
1843, and again during the four weeks, that I preached to you as a candidate, in Nov. and Dec., 1844, I lec-
tured in the city twice on the immediate abolition of
of Slavery; once, on the paramount importance of an
improved system of popular Instruction; and once,
if I remember correctly, on the great expediency, if
not duty, of Total Abstinence from the use of any intoxicating drinks. Therefore if you have been much
disappointed in the character of my ministry here,
you must blame your want of discernment, and not
any concealment on my part.

But, dear friends, neither you nor I foresaw the demands, that have been made upon me in this city—
the trials of my faith; the tests of my fidelity.

I found myself here within a few miles of the rem-
nant of a once noble tribe of Indians. The condition
and fate of the Aborigines of the American Conti-
nent, had long been a subject of painful interest to
me. I could not bear to hear them spoken of as an

effete race; destined to extermination, as fast as the superior races of men shall come on to take possession of the lands, they will not cultivate, the mines they will not work, and the water-powers they will not improve. It seemed to me that great pains should be taken to develope them individually and socially; to help them unfold the nature, that God has given them, in which we see traits enough like our own to assure us they are human, and therefore capable of becoming partakers of the divine. I therefore felt it incumbent on me to proffer these neighbors of ours any assistance, I might be able to render them. I helped them raise the means to build a meeting-house, a school-house, and a double tenement for the accommodation of the missionary and a school teacher. I procured for them nearly twenty years ago a good instructor for their children; obtained from the Superintendent of Public Instruction an annual appropriation for her support, and the support of her successors to the present time; and for several years I visited the school frequently. I obtained first from benevolent individuals donations of money, and subsequently, for a number of years, have received from a Boston Society for the propagation of the Gospel, an annual appropriation to aid in the support of the Mission, established there by the Methodist Conference. In various ways, I have devoted a great many hours to my Indian friends. For three years past I have been obliged to bestow very much less attention upon them than formerly. Still their applications for advice, or aid of some kind, are more numerous than the weeks of the year. Some slight improvements in their condition are apparent. But not until the tenure of their lands is changed; not until the Reservation is sub-divided among the families of the Tribe; and the fruits of their industry or skill shall be secured to the workers and their descendants,*—not until then will the Indians be brought to feel those inducements to labor, which have impelled white men to subdue the earth, and make even "the wilderness to blossom like the rose."

Another large class of suffering, neglected human beings—*the Canal Boys*—soon after I came here, attracted my notice, and awakened my sympathy. Living on James street, I had occasion to pass and re-pass over the bridges every day; and scarcely ever did I pass them, that I did not see some evidence of the loathsome condition of the thousands of boys employed upon this great thoroughfare of our internal navigation; or hear from their own lips profanity or obsceneness. The casual inquiries, that I made about them, excited my compassion all the more, as they brought to my view their condition of not a little physical hardship and abuse, and of utter intellectual and moral neglect. My feelings soon were vented in the hearing of those, who promptly and cordially responded to them in acts, as well as words. About the first of December, 1845, I was kindly invited by the Rev. Dr. Adams, then Pastor of the First Presbyterian Church, to take tea and spend the evening at his house, with the other ministers of the town. We had a very pleasant interview; conversed at length about the state and prospects of our country, and especially the condition of the community, in which we were laboring. Towards the close of the evening, I laid upon them the burden of my thoughts respecting the Canal Boys; what I had heard of their wrongs

---

* See Appendix "M."

and their exposure; and what it seemed to me should be done for their protection, and improvement. The subject was taken up gladly by all present, and well considered. Dr. Adams, Rev. Mr. Taggart then of the Baptist Church, and myself were appointed a Committe, to prepare a Memorial to the Legislature; call a public meeting, as soon as it should seem to us advisable, and bring the subject to the consideration of our fellow citizens. In pursuance of this action of the ministers, a large meeting, comprising many of the most respectable citizens of the town, was held on the 15th of December following, in the First Presbyterian Church. The Memorial was read, eloquently advocated, and unanimously adopted, praying the Legislature to pass such an Act, as would secure to the Canal Boys protection to their persons and compensation for services; homes and suitable instruction in the winters for that large portion of them, who were parentless; and a Reformatory for those, who should beome delinquents. We opened an extensive correspondence with prominent philanthropists, and men of influence along the lines of the Canals in the State; another meeting was held in the Presbyterian Church on the 29th of December, and a third meeting of our citizens in January. Our Memorial was numerously signed here and in many other places. It was presented and earnestly advocated by several members of both Houses of our General Assembly. But, I am sorry and ashamed to add, the only part of our plan that was adopted and enacted by the Legislature, resulted in the institution of the Reform School at Rochester, which, if the reports I have heard have any measure of truth in them, has not been conducted on the best principles to effect the purpose of such a School.

Soon after, I was called to assist, and did what I could in this town and many other parts of the county, to enable the Managers of our Orphan Asylum to purchase the large building, which it now occupies, and extend greatly the usefulness of that beneficent institution.

The cause of Temperance, I need not tell you, has always had my cordial support here as elsewhere. And I have done, what I have been able to do, for the improvement of our System of Public Instruction in this city and in many parts of the State. I have delivered many lectures on the subject, and have often assisted at Teachers' Institutes, and Educational Conventions.

Here let me disclose what to most of you may be a secret. In 1846 or 47, a meeting was called, through the newspapers, of all those, who were in favor of instituting a course of Popular Lectures. Only two persons beside myself heeded the Call.* Not to be balked of a good purpose, we modestly called ourselves (as was reported in the newspapers) a meeting of respectable citizens of Syracuse. Mr. Raymond was chosen Chairman, Mr. Gardner, Secretary. I made (of course an eloquent) speech on the importance of the object, for which the meeting had been called, and moved a series of Resolutions, that were (also of course) unanimously adopted. A committee was appointed, composed of the gentlemen present, and of two others who we knew, would co-operate with us to make the necessary arrangements for a Course of

* Rev. R. R. Raymond and Geo. J. Gardner, Esq.

Popular Lectures, to be delivered in our City Hall, the ensuing winter, tickets 12½ cents.

Our doings were published. We made up a Corps of Lecturers, partly from among the able men of our own city, or village as it then was, and partly from those of other parts of the country. The undertaking was so successful, that we continued to do likewise for two or three years. This revived the Franklin Institute. Into the hands of that organization, we resigned the charge of our Popular Lectures, which were well provided for, until within the last three years. I will not forbear to express my very deep regret, that the Managers of the Institute have seen fit to discontinue their Lectures, and substitute for them the nightly enactment, for three or four weeks, of Farces, not always, I fear, of a high order—not often improving, if they are always innocently amusing.

But another matter of greatest moment, it will not be denied, has occupied much of my time and thought. The very Spring, that I came to reside with you, was pending the annexation of Texas for the obvious, and not concealed, purpose of extending the domains of the Slaveholders; and confirming their ascendancy in the government of our nation. Before the close of 1845, that most nefarious plot was consummated. And the next year, as a necessary sequel, our utterly unjustifiable war was waged with Mexico. As a lover of my country, friend of humanity, a hater of oppression, I could not be, and, as you know, I was not silent, either in the pulpit or out of it. Some of my parishioners, and more of our neighbors, I am aware condemned my course; objected that I was introducing politics into the Sacred Desk. My answer here was the same, that it had been elsewhere; "if inculcating the two Great Commandments, and the Golden Rule be preaching politics; if reiterating the glorious Declaration of our national Fathers, that 'all men are created equal,' and denouncing every violation of the inalienable rights of 'the least of our brethren,' be preaching politics; then woe is me, and woe to every other man, who stands before the people as a minister of the Gospel, and does not preach politics; and woe to the church, the statesman, and the nation, that will not give good heed to such preaching." The terrible visitation of Providence in our civil war, (not yet I fear wholly past,) has shown to us and the world, that the mightiest nation may not, any more than the humblest individual, with impunity set at naught the law of God, and the claims of humanity. It may be, that I recurred to this subject oftener than was necessary; but that were better than not to have spoken.

The business of the Under-ground Rail-road, with which I had been connected since 1830, was much increased by the alarm of the Southern slaves, lest they should be driven into the newly acquired territory of their masters. And though it cost me a great deal of time, not a little money, and sometimes a sleepless night, I could not refuse always to act as a Director, and not unfrequently as a Conductor of those, who were fleeing from cruel bondage.

Moreover, when in 1850, our United States Congress enacted the atrocious Fugitive Slave Act; and my Unitarian brother, Millard Fillmore, made it the Law of the land by giving it his signature; and the once revered Daniel Webster came here, and went elsewhere, enjoining upon the people obedience to that Law; and so many prominent Northern civilians

and ministers, some of my own religious denomination,
insisted that we ought to conform to the Law, I could
not but take for my text the words of Peter (Acts v.
29,) "We ought to obey God rather than men," and
harp upon it in season and out of season. I did sum-
mon you, and all within the hearing of my voice, to
withstand that Law, at any cost, at every hazard, if
need be, " to the death."* I did spend much time in
Conventions, and smaller meetings, and in lecturing
about the country, doing all in my power to rouse the
people to resist the Fugitive Slave Law.

When, therefore, (in fulfilment of the prediction
of Mr. Webster,) in the midst of an anti-slavery
meeting in this City, on the 1st of Oct. 1851, an un-
offending man, who had lived here a number of years,
getting an honest living by his useful handicraft, was
claimed as a slave, seized, handcuffed to be borne
away with the sanction of a United States officer, I
joined in the cry " *to the rescue ;*" and lent my hand
to effect it. In another place,† I hope ere long to give
a more full account of this transaction, than would be
pertinent here. Let me only add now, that I have not
lived long enough yet, to be ashamed of anything I
said, or did, for " the Rescue of Jerry."

And what shall I say more of the " naughty deeds"
and " extraneous subjects" as they have been considered by many, which for the last twenty-two years,
have engrossed so much of the time and thought of
your minister, that ought to have been devoted, some
may say, more immediately to your service? I can
think of no other but " Woman's Rights."

Soon after the commencement of the Anti-Slavery

* See Appendix, " M."
† Christian Register, Boston. Anti-Slavery Recollections.

Reform, I had delivered in Providence, R. I., a Lecture on the condition of the enslaved millions of our countrymen, as it was according to the laws of the States and of the Republic. A most estimable and intelligent lady, who was one of my auditors, begged to know, if I was indifferent to the fact, or ignorant, that there were millions of my fellow beings in the Northern States, whose condition, *according to law*, was not much better than that of the Southern slaves. I confessed my ignorance, and insisted that such could not be the case, and I not know it. She then ran a parallel between the legal condition of females at the North and that of the slaves at the South, which surprised and shocked me. I promised her that I would be ignorant and indifferent no longer. And ever since that hour, I confess the "Rights of Woman" have been often under my consideration, and frequently the subject of consideration and public discourse.

In 1846, the citizens of this State were summoned to the Polls, to declare by vote their opinions and wishes, relative to the sale of intoxicating drinks—whether they would, or would not, have a "Prohibitory Law." But the larger portion of the people—*the women*—although their happiness and comfort were so much impaired—often utterly destroyed by the prevalent intemperance of their husbands, brothers or sons, were not allowed to influence directly the decision.

In the same year, our nation was plunged into the miseries and crimes of as wicked a war as was ever waged. But the women, though they have to bear an equal, if not a greater, part of the miseries incident to war, were not allowed to assist by their votes in the election of such men to office, in our National Government, as would have averted that dire calamity, and compound of crimes.

But more flagrant still was the injustice to woman brought to my most painful consideration, that same year, when the new Constitution of the State—the fundamental law of our political being—the law affecting so vitally the prosperity, the liberty, the lives of women as well as men—when the Constitution of New York, as it had been revised and amended that year, was submitted to the acceptance or rejection of the people, *and the better half of them*—the women— were not permitted to manifest their approval or disapproval; to give or withhold *their consent* to the government, to which they were to be subjected. This series, this quick succession of wrongs, roused me, as never before, to espouse " the Rights of Woman." In the fall of 1846, I preached and published my first sermon, devoted wholly to this subject; and committed myself before my country and the world to the demand of the full enfranchisement of the Female Sex, equal pecuniary, legal, conjugal, political rights. That sermon has been published and re-published in this country, and in England, more times than any other writing I have ever given to the press. By all the reflection I have bestowed upon the subject since, I am fully confirmed in my conviction of the correctness of the prominent positions taken in that discourse. And I am fully persuaded, that never will our governments be well and truly, wisely and happily enacted and administered, until we have *mothers* as well as *fathers* of the State.*

Dear Friends, members of this Church, it cannot be

---

* See Appendix "N."

doubted, if I had not paid so much attention to the numerous matters, of which I have now spoken, that I should have given more attention to you individually and collectively—to your families and your children. And, although you have borne with me so patiently, and judged me so leniently, and many of you have sympathised, encouraged and co-operated with me so generously in most, if not all, of my labors;—although dear Friends, I see and feel, that you are not disposed to reproach me in my old age, so near the natural, and, if you see fit, the earlier termination of my ministry to you—although you have always been so patient with me; yet I frankly confess, that I am not satisfied with my services to you ; and acknowledge that you have reason to be not satisfied. In the searching review I have given to the almost twenty-three years past, I see some things that I seriously regret. For, though I still believe, that a Minister of the Gospel ought to be quite as earnest, as I have been, in the advocacy of the equal, natural civil and political rights of men and women, without regard to complexion ; and ought to do as much, and more than I have done, in the cause of Peace, of Temperance and Popular Education ; yet are there other things, more immediately promotive of the improvement and prosperity of a Church, which no minister should leave undone, so much as I have. All my omissions and mistakes I intend frankly to confess to you, if permitted to do so, on another occasion. And I shall most earnestly warn my successor against them, if I live to see him. Would that I could by my own exertions, make all the reparation, that I see to be due to you. But I am now an old man—unable to labor as I would, and as I once could, for you. I am three score years and ten ; and although

I do not feel that this is, what the text intimates it to be, the limit of man's life on earth; yet the second part of the passage admonishes that, however strong I may now feel, I must expect soon a decline of all my powers.

You, dear Friends, may perceive such a decline already; and may have come to feel the need of a younger and abler minister. Now therefore, as I have long intended to do, if I should live to be seventy—I tender to you, Trustees and Members of this Church, *my resignation.* Accept it immediately, if you prefer; or let it take effect, whenever you may have engaged the services of another, to whom you may be disposed to commit the office, you have so long entrusted to me. And may the God of all wisdom, purity and grace, guide your choice to one, who shall be eminently qualified to lead you to the knowledge of all essential truth, and quicken you continually in the divine life., that life, of which Jesus of Nazareth was so perfect a pattern.

APPENDIX.

------◆------

[A.]

The American Peace, The American Temperance, The American Anti-Slavery Society, I know commenced in Boston. That city was also the birth place of the Bethel and Seaman's Aid Societies ; of city missions ; and of schools for the Reformation of Juvenile Delinquents. There too commenced the Asylums for the Insane, for the Blind and Idiotic ; and Normal Schools for the careful thorough preparation of Teachers. If I am not misinformed, the germs of the American Bible and Foreign Missionary Societies were started also in Boston. Now I do not claim that all these philanthropic enterprises originated with Unitarians, though five of them did. But the significant fact to which I would point the attention of my readers is, that in that region, where alone the Unitarian Theology has ever been in the ascendant, there these devices and attempts for the benefit of the ignorant, suffering and sinning classes were commenced or suggested.

[B.]

Soon after the outbreak of the American Revolution, the Rector of Kings Chapel, left the country with other loyalists. The Church thus deprived of its pastor, invited James Freeman, who had just commenced his studies preparatory to the Episcopal Ministry, to conduct, as a Reader, their services of public worship. In the then distracted state of the country, and with few, if any ministers of that denomination near him, Mr. Freeman, was left pretty much to himself, in his researches after the truth as it is in Jesus. At the close of the war, the Vestry and Wardens of Kings Chapel proposed to put their house in order, and secure to themselves and children all the advantages of a fully appointed ministry. So they quite unanimously invited Mr. Freeman, to become their Rector. He accepted the call, and went into Connecticut, where the Bishop of the diocese resided, to receive ordination. On examination by that high official, it was found that the young man could not subscribe to the Thirty-nine Articles, without such qualifictions of their literal meaning as amounted, the Bishop thought to a contradiction of some of them. With all his careful thorough study of the Bible (and Mr. Freeman, was an excellent scholar,) he

had failed to find in it the Trinity, the Foreordination of a portion of
the human race to salvation, and the rest to damnation, or the doctrine of the Atonement by the vicarious punishment of Christ. So
ordination was refused him. He returned to Boston, to inform his
astonished friends, that he was accounted a heretic, an unbeliever,
unfit to be a minister of Christianity. They requested him to give
them a full exposition of his religious and theological opinions. He
did so and these were so acceptable to the Wardens and a large majority
of the Vestry, that they determined to have Mr. Freeman, for pastor,
the Bishop's refusal to consecrate him notwithstanding. Accordingly
they ordained the young man themselves, in as solemn and impressive
a manner as the Bishop could have done it. They published a new
edition of the Book of Common Prayer, omitting the Thirty-nine articles and the Athanasian, and Nicene Creeds, and all expressions implying the Deity of Jesus; and retained in all other particulars the
Liturgy of the Episcopal Church. Thus origanated the first Unitarian
Church in our country. In that church it was my privilege to be
brought up.

[C.]

Soon after I had commenced the study of Theology, and the critical
examination of the Bible, I came to doubt the miraculous conception
of Jesus, the truth of which I had always taken for granted. Alarmed
at what seemed to me then a tendency to skepticism, I went to see Dr.
Ware, and asked for a private interview; determined if, after he
should be informed of the character and state of my mind, he should
so advise me (as I expected he might) that I would take up my connection with the Divinity School, and turn to some Secular occupation.
With considerable emotion I disclosed to him my doubt; and the
difficulty I found in reconciling different passages of the Sacred Scrip-
ture with each other, and with commonly received opinions on other
subjects. After a full and frank exposure of my mind and its thought,
I awaited anxiously his reply. In his kindest manner, he said, "Mr.
May, I am glad that you have arrived at a doubt. It shows me that
you have entered upon your new course of study in a proper spirit,
determined to be thorough and faithful, and not take doctrines upon
trust, because they are commonly received and popular." But, I re-
joined, how Sir, would you remove this doubt, and relieve my difficulty?
He replied, "I could not probably solve this doubt for you, if I would;
I would not if I could, at present. It will be better for you to grapple
with the difficulty yourself; pursue the examination of the subject
much farther than you have done; and seek a solution, that will be
satisfactory to your own mind and heart." I inquired if he did not consider the doctrine a very important, if not a vital one. "Nothing, he

said, is so important to you, as to be faithful in your endeavors to learn the truth, and be 'fully persuaded in your own mind,' that what you believe is true. And no belief is of vital consequence, but that which shall lead, impel you to fear God, and keep his commandments. Go on earnestly, thoroughly, prayerfully in your studies, your inquiries, not doubting, that the Father of your spirit will lead you to the knowledge of all essential truth."

[D.]

I was traveling with one of my sisters, in an old fashioned stage-coach. Somewhere between Baltimore and Washington, we saw by the roadside twenty or thirty colored men, handcuffed and fastened along a heavy chain, that was attached to a wagon. "What have these men been doing, what crime have they committed?" exclaimed my sister. "O said a fellow passenger, they are only a gang of slaves that some planter or trader has purchased; and he is taking them on South." "Is this the way slaves are treated in our country," she replied. I joined with her in expressing our shame and horror. "You must be from the North" said a gentleman on the back seat, "from New England perhaps, not used to seeing slaves." "Yes Sir," I replied "we are from Massachusetts; and I never so fully realized before how great a privilege it is to live where human beings cannot be treated in this manner." He courteously dropped the subject; and so did I, but it dropped into the bottom of my heart, and made me an Abolitionist.

[E.]

I was greatly assisted in my labors in the cause of Peace, by a most excellent gentleman—Mr. George Benson, who had retired from business in Providence; and had removed with his family to live on a farm in Brooklyn. He had been connected with "the Society of Friends" and was an earnest advocate of their pacific principles. He brought me acquainted with several of the best authors on the subject; and did much to confirm my opinions and encourage my efforts. "Peace to his blessed memory."

We received from some English friends of Peace, a remarkable pamphlet by Jonathan Dymond, entitled "An Inquiry into the accordancy of war with the principles of Christianity." This Tract revealed to me a mind so in harmony, and sympathy with the mind of Jesus, that I procured a copy of his "Essays on the Principles of Morality," in two volumes. With these I was so fully satisfied, that, in 1834, I procured, through the agency of my friend, Rev. George Bush, of New York, the republication of them by Messrs. Harper & Brothers. I would earnestly commend them to the attentive perusal of all, who would thoroughly understand "the righteousness of Christ."

[F.]

It is with pleasure I here record my testimony to the very valuable services to the cause of Temperance rendered, at that early day, by John Frost, Esq. He had been a lawyer of considerable distinction at the Bar of Windham County ; but so alarmed had he become at the ravages of Intemperance in our country, that he left his profession and devoted himself for years, I believe, for the rest of his life to pleading with his fellow men, near and far, to abstain wholly from the use of intoxicating drinks.

Here too, I must be allowed to make a grateful mention of another gentleman, who did good service—Vine Robinson, Esq. of Brooklyn. He was for several years one of the associate Judges of the County Court. But he had never ventured to make a speech in public, until he had become so deeply interested in the cause of Temperance, that he could keep silence no longer. He rose one evening, and to his own surprise, more even than to that of his neighbors, showed that the soul of eloquence was in him. Afterwards he went about addressing, with great effect, small audiences and large.

[G.]

I have been informed by the Hon. Henry Barnard, Editor of the American Journal of Education, that the Convention which was called in Brooklyn, was the first Convention ever held in the Country to consider the condition of the Common Schools ; and propose the improvement of them.

In our Circular of invitation, we put quite a number of questions, the answers to which would bring out the information we desired, respecting the character of the Schools throughout Connecticut. Those questions were answered either by delegates in person, or by letters from more than a hundred towns, and they disclosed such a general indifference to the schools, that the publication of the report of the Convention surprised and mortified the better part of the people of the State, and led to the commencement of essential improvements.

[H.]

I did not enlarge, in my discourse, upon my connection with Mr. Garrison, and the Anti Slavery Reform which he commenced, though the most important episode in the history of my life, because I have published within the last year, in the Christian Register of Boston, a series of articles on this great conflict for liberty in our land. I expect to publish a dozen or twenty more of my Anti Slavery Recollections, and then republish the whole in a volume, which I hope will issue from the press before the middle of January next.

[I.]

One of the many interesting memories I have of my residence in Brooklyn, is the intimate acquaintance and friendship, I there formed with the late Rev. Frederick T. Gray. He had been for a number of years a successful book merchant in Boston. But the desire of his heart, from early youth, had been to devote himself to the Gospel Ministry, especially to the poor. He early associated himself with that eminent servant of God, the pious Dr. Tuckerman, in his work as a City Missionary; and rendered inestimable services, as the Principal of a large Sunday School for the children of the poor. But circumstances, which he could not surmount, forbade his becoming *a preacher*, until the year 1830, when by the Will of a deceased relative he was put in possession of a moderate fortune. As soon as practicable after the receipt of his legacy, he settled up his business; came to Brooklyn, and for a year or more studied Divinity under my direction. His heart was so unfeignedly engaged in the work of the Lord, that he made rapid progress in his preparation for the pulpit; and at the expiration of about twelve months, he returned to Boston; was ordained, in 1833, and become so acceptable a preacher, that, after several years ministry in Pitts Street Chapel, he was called to Bulfinch Street Church in 1839. Thence he went in 1853 on a mission to California, to the newly established Unitarian Church in San Francisco. He returned from that city the following year, and died in Boston, March, 1855, with the testimony of all, who had known him, that his whole life had been a christian ministry.

[J.]

I have spoken in my discourse of Miss Caroline Tilden; well known to all who were pupils or instructors in the Normal School first in Lexington, afterwards at West Newton, as "the bright, particular star" in that constellation. I discovered her genius, while she was the modest mistress of a village school in South Scituate. I induced her to go to the Normal School at Bridgewater; having readily obtained from a wealthy gentleman—Mr. N. C. Nash—who knew her well, the means to defray her expenses at that Institution for a couple of years. Under the instruction of that thorough teacher Col. Tillinghast, she perfected her knowledge of the fundamental branches of Science, taught in Common Schools; and prepared herself to be, what she afterwards was, the inspiring genius of many, who were seeking to acquire the "art of teaching."

Another delightful recollection of my six happy years in South Scituate is, that there too I found her brother, now the Rev. Wm. P. Tilden of Boston, and helped him, in a course of three years study, out of a ship-yard, where he was accounted an excellent workman, into the pulpit where he has done since 1840, and is doing, invaluable service.

[K.]

I should have come to reside in Syracuse, several months sooner than I did, but for a serious, vexatious difficulty, in which the churches of Lexington had been involved for twenty years or more, respecting a large fund for the support of the Ministry of the town. The fund was created by subscriptions and donations at an early day, when there was only one Church there. But in process of time differences of theological belief had arisen amongst the people ; and churches of several denominations had been gathered. Each of these claimed a share of the Fund. It became the subject of repeated litigation. The decisions of the Courts and of the Legislature, to whom at length the matter was carried—were, that the income of the Fund legally belonged to the old original Church. But the claimants were not satisfied, and discord and strife continued. When I became the temporary minister of the Old Society, I looked into the matter, and became satisfied that, if the Law gave the fund wholly to that Church, christian equity did not ; and that there would never be peace and good-fellowship among the people of the different churches, until the income of the fund should be equitably divided. I was confident that what ought to be done, could be done. I was allowed to devise the plan of settlement, and remained there long enough to see it accomplished.

[L.]

While I was endeavoring to gather a Unitarian Church in Hartford, Rev. Dr. Hawes—then the most distinguished Orthodox minister in that city, delivered a number of lectures upon the history, character and doctrines of the Fathers of New England. In the course of these lectures, he made a very severe attack upon Unitarianism. I heard it, and, the following evening replied to it before a large audience, as well as I was able at so short a notice. The lectures were afterwards published in a volume, entitled a "Tribute to the Memory of the Pilgrims." I then carefully prepared and published a Review of his work, in a pamphlet of 72 octavo pages—the largest theological writing of mine, that has ever been printed.

[M.]*

Good Capt. Oliver Teall, whom I had tried in vain to convert to my pacific principles, though he was a peace-loving man, as well as an ardent friend of temperance-kindly upbraided me for what he considered

my inconsistency, in counselling determined opposition to the Fugitive
Slave Law. But I only insisted, that all good men and true ought to
withstand the execution of that infamous Law, in the way and by the
means, they each one of them conscientiously believed to be right.
I declared that I had no confidence in the use of deadly weapons, that
I would not carry even my cane to the rescue of one, who should be
seized under the Law. I would *hold* a man who was attempting to ex-
ecute it, if I could ; overpower him if I had strength so to do ; but not
intentionally harm a hair of his head. Nevertheless, I did solemnly
enjoin it upon those, who believed it right, in the sight of God, for
them to fight for their own liberty, or for the liberty of a white brother;
I did enjoin it upon them, (if it should seem necessary,) to fight for
the rescue of any black man, from the horrors of a return into Slavery.

[N.]

On this subject of Woman's ;Rights, allow me here to commend to
my readers the numerous publications, that have issued from the press
in this country, and in England, during the last twenty years. They
are worthy the most profound consideration of all, who wish to see
exhibited a perfect example of a Nation, governed by "the people, "
not by a Nobility, nor an Aristocracy, nor any other favored class,
but by "the people ; " by "the consent of all the governed," who are
of adult age, and sane minds, and are not known to have been guity of
crime. Such a Government, a true Christian Democracy, is yet to be
instituted. It never can exist until woman shall be enfranchised. I
particularly commend the Speeches and Appeals of Mrs. Elizabeth
Cady Stanton, of Wendell Phillips, and Theodore Parker, and
Lucretia Motte, and Anna E. Dickenson ; and the writings of Mrs.
Caroline H. Dall, and Mrs. Farnham, and Mrs. Gage, of our County,
and Mrs. Mill, in the Westminster Review of England, and more
especially, the late masterly speeches of John Stuart Mill, in the Par-
liament of Great Britain, and of George William Curtis, in the Con-
stitutional Convention at Albany.

[O.]

I would here append a few words to the paragraph, ending in the
middle of the 38th page. No one, who knows me, would suspect that
I am opposed to Amusements. The animal spirits of children, and the
young, will impel them to some things besides the sober occupations of
life ; and it were vain to attempt to withhold them from all amusement.
Then the adage is undoubtedly true, "all work and no play makes

* The reference to this letter on page 35, is an error.

52

Jack a dull boy." And older people often need relaxation from the labors and cares of life, *recreation*. It is obviously, then, the part of wisdom to take cognizance of this fact. The friends of morality and true religion should, as far as possible, take the "amusements" of the community into their own hands ; see to it that enough of them, and of the right kinds, are provided, and had in proper places, and in due measure. Parents especially, whose children are wont to associate, should confer much together, and co-operate in the endeavor to procure for their children enough proper amusements, under proper regulations. In 1846, I preached and published a sermon on the subject, which was severely censured, at that time by some of my neighbors, who probably, in this day, would approve of the advice given therein.

www.ingramcontent.com/pod-product-compliance
Lightning Source LLC
Chambersburg PA
CBHW031806090426
42739CB00008B/1182